My Artwork

Rhea Gupta

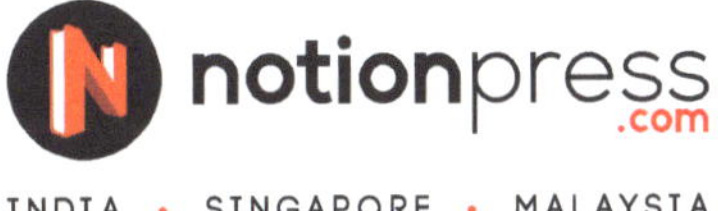

INDIA · SINGAPORE · MALAYSIA

History of Art by Rhea Gupta

The history of art has evolved from ancient time to present.

At the early ages, the art was only evident in cave paintings. Today, it is everywhere, advertisements, museums, and merchandise.

It can be tracked in the form of colours, shapes, geometry, symmetry and also styles of medium of painting. There is a special cultural significance of painting in India. It can be gold gilded, godly or even commercial.

The contemporary painting in India is very fashionable and inn.

According to me, the best contemporary creative arts are calligraphy, gold gilding, acrylic/oil/watercolour painting, clay modelling, inking, also shading, sketching and colouring.

Paints in today's time can be manufactured at home using pigments and gums that are specially used industrially and commercially as well.

The best paints are most expensive while they can be handmade or machine made.

Colours and shapes play an important role in the design of a painting or drawing as the more bigger a shape the more bright it appears and the more interesting/small a shape, the darker it appears just like gems. That is why jewellery is so intricate and complex looking.

The more one experiences the colour and shades of different drawings and paintings, the better one gets at choosing colour harmony and defining the reason for or justly so to say "the outline and beauty of an artist's perspective".

The character of a painting is defined by the subject it is meant to express. A painting might be gorgeous/comical/pattern/colourful or even simply natural.

The best paintings are those that may be eye catching but are parallel to the perspectives of a person. For example, one painting might be good for a person but not so good for another so it's subjective.

However, for an artist all painting are a masterpiece as long as they are colourful or gray but they should be full of colours.

Art is a subject through which anyone can express their opinion and view of life and environment.

Thanks;
Rhea Gupta
9th May 2025

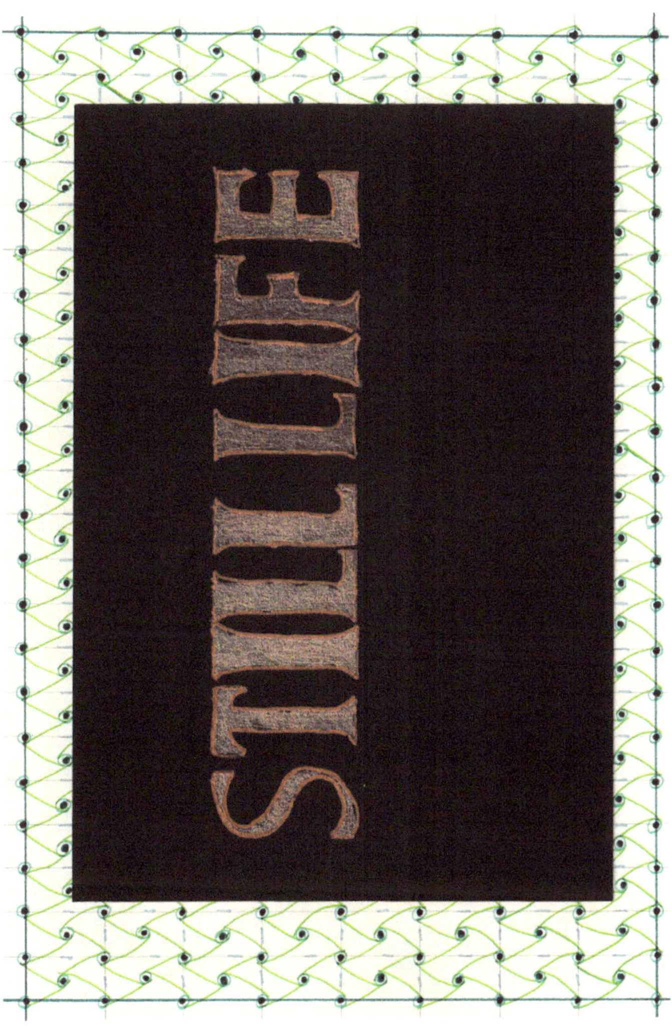
STILL LIFE

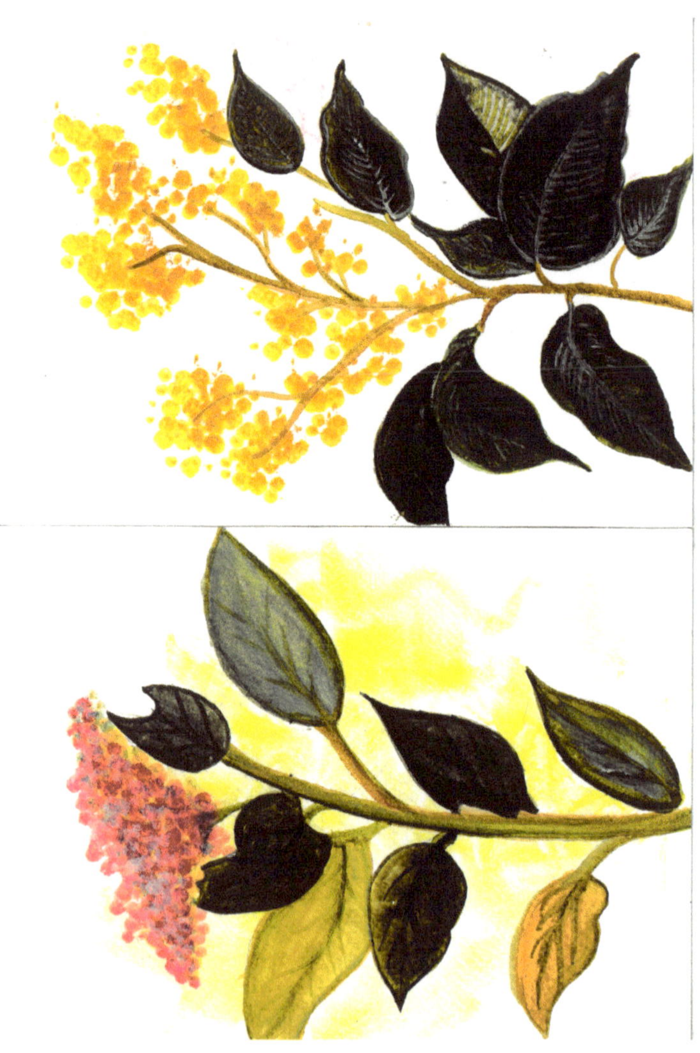

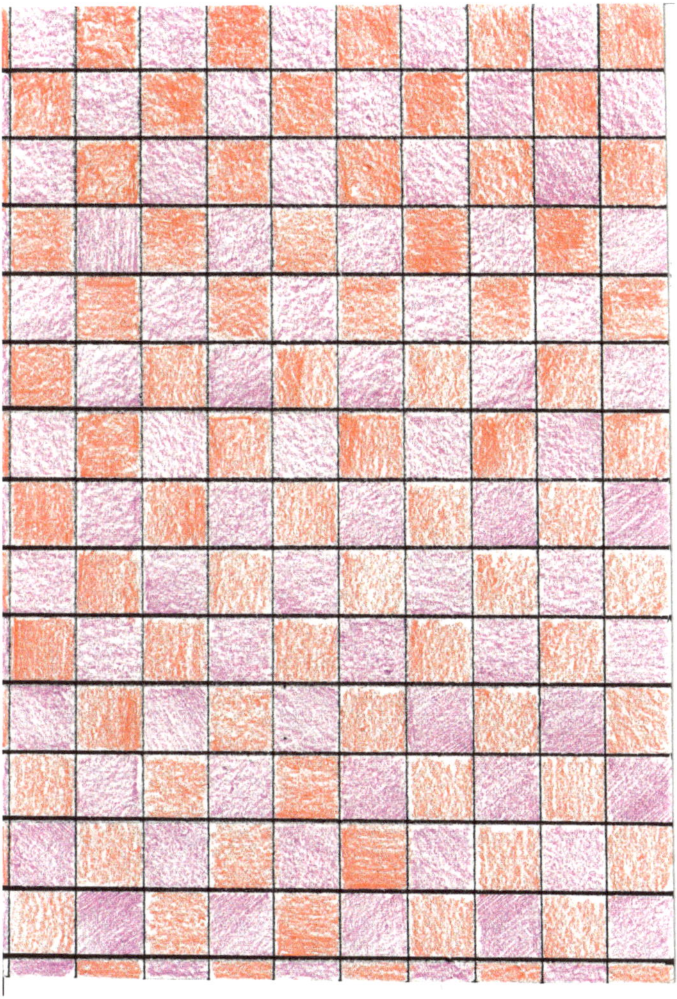

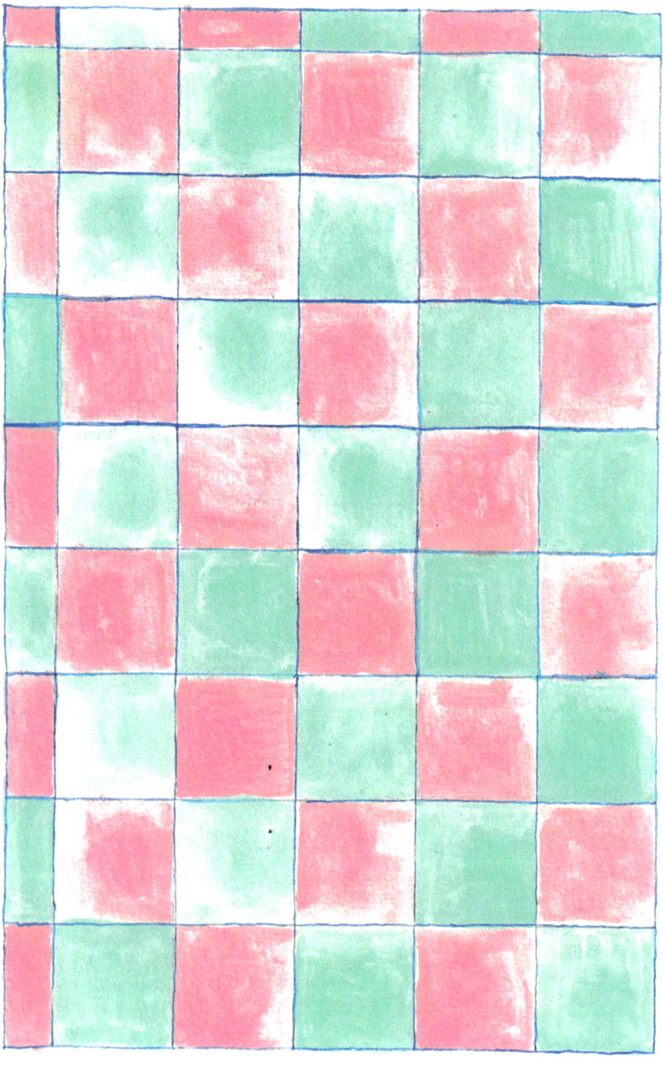

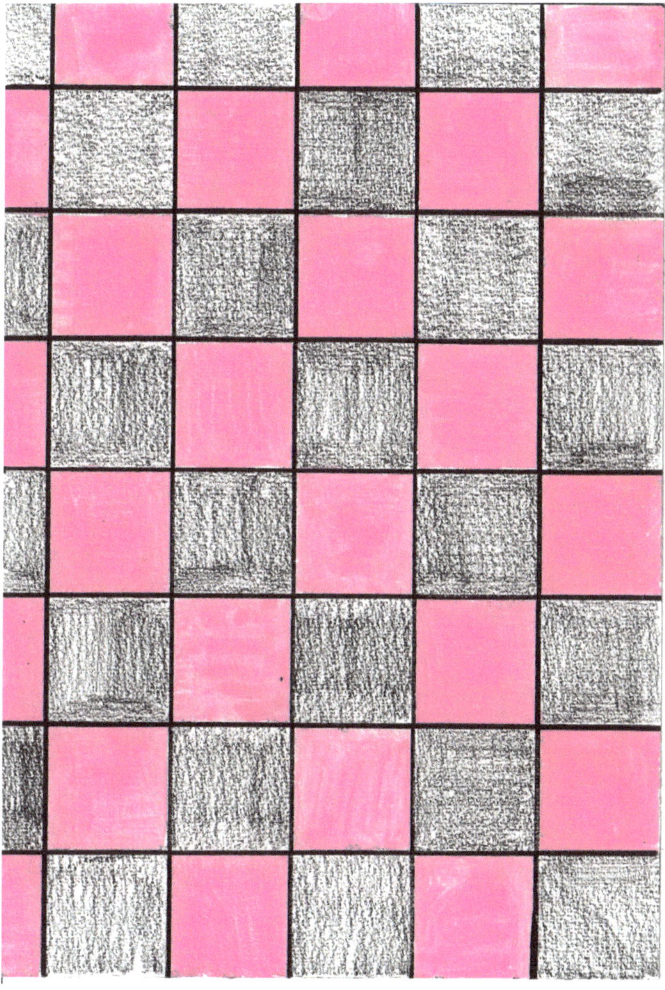

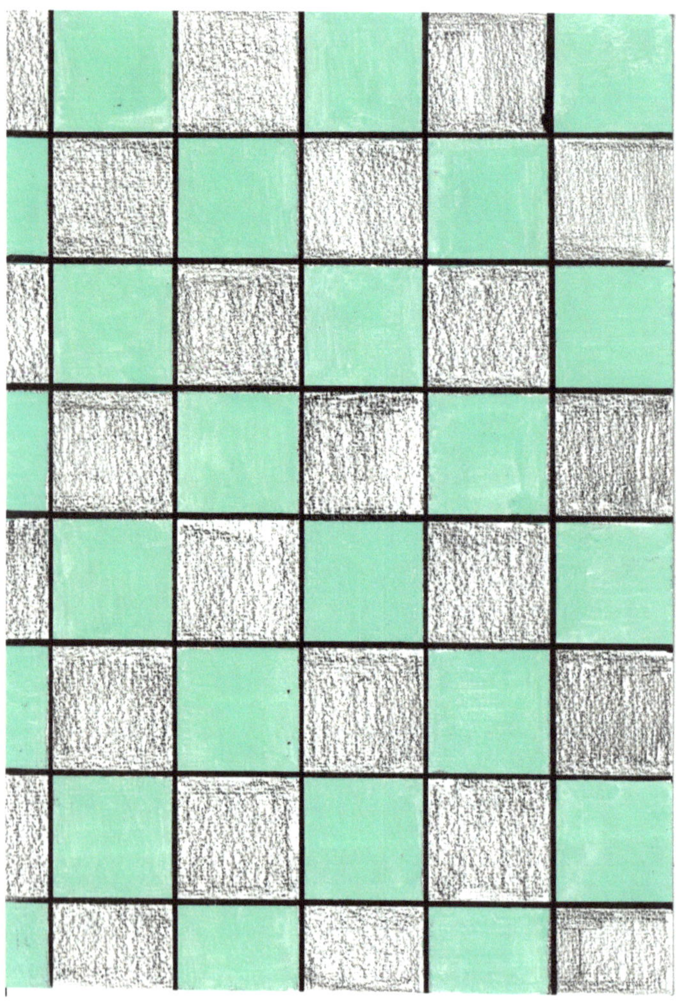

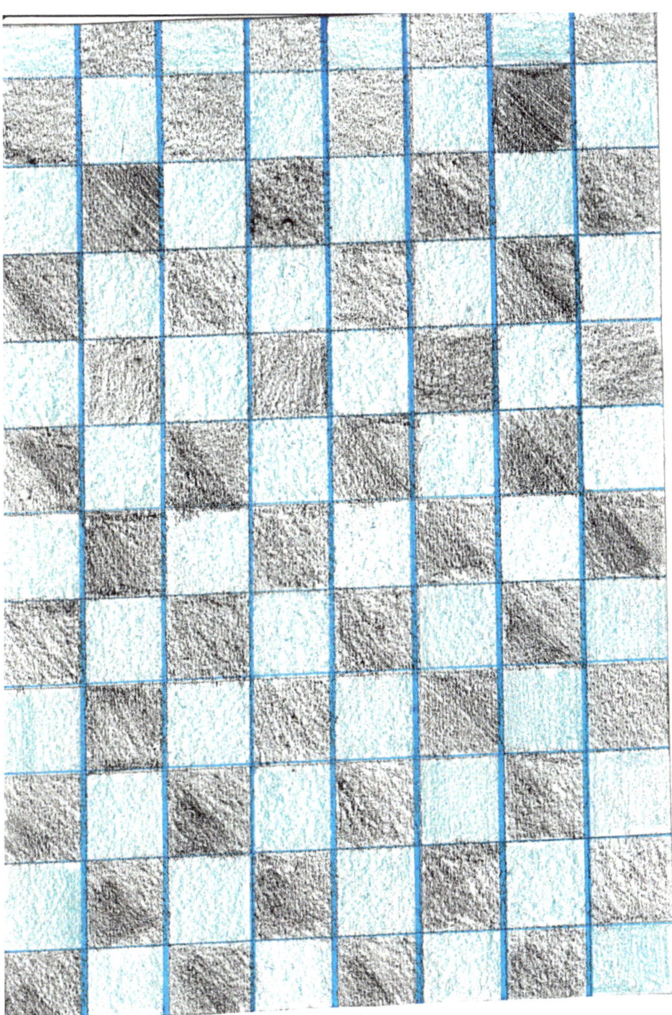

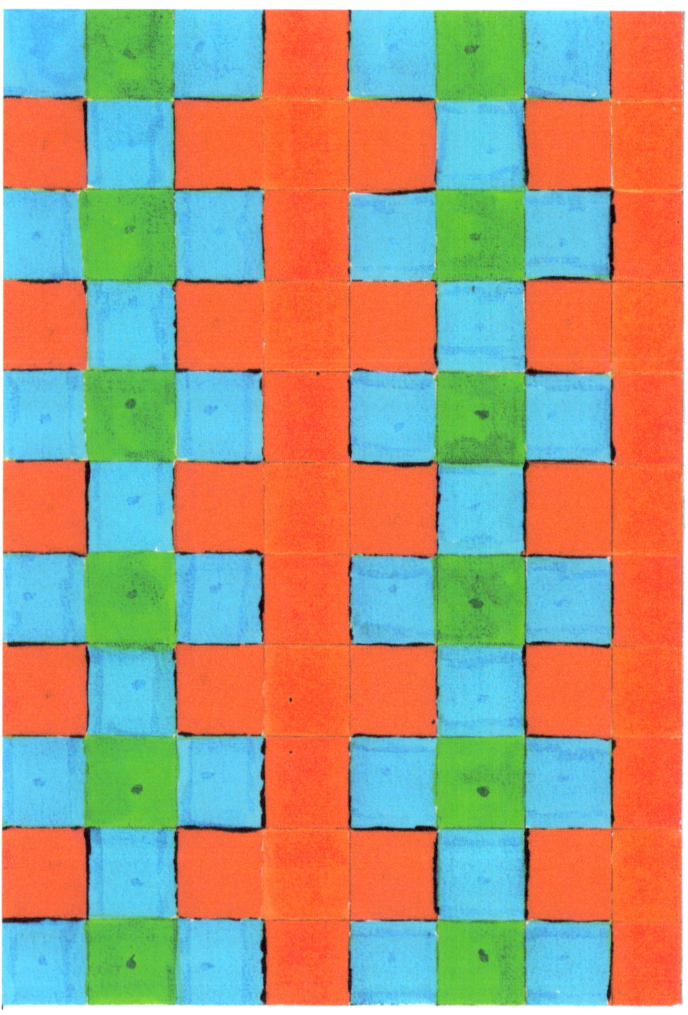

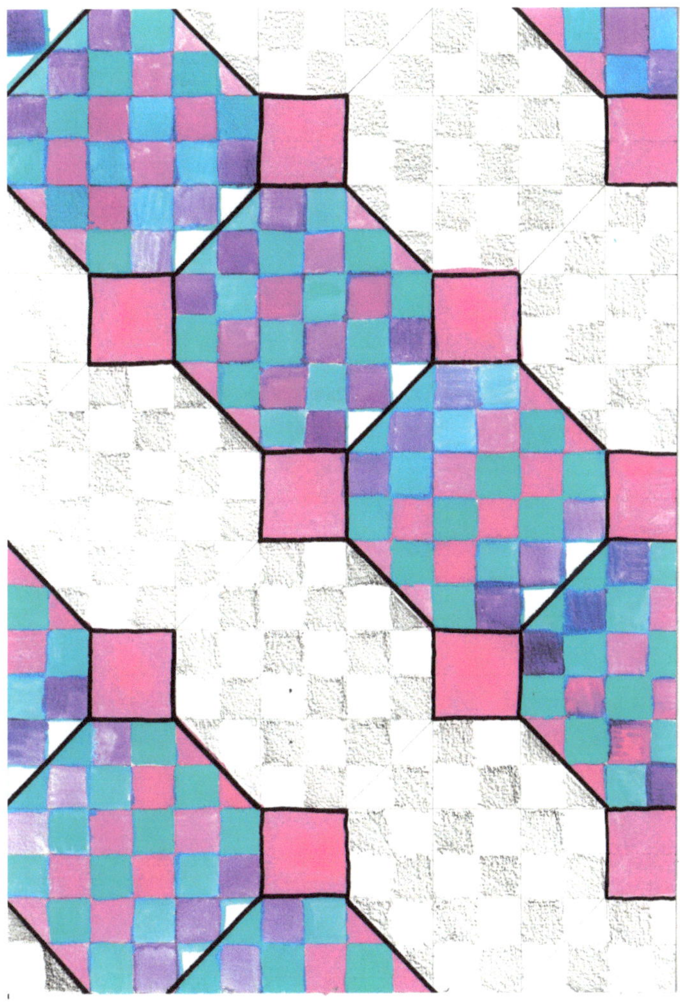

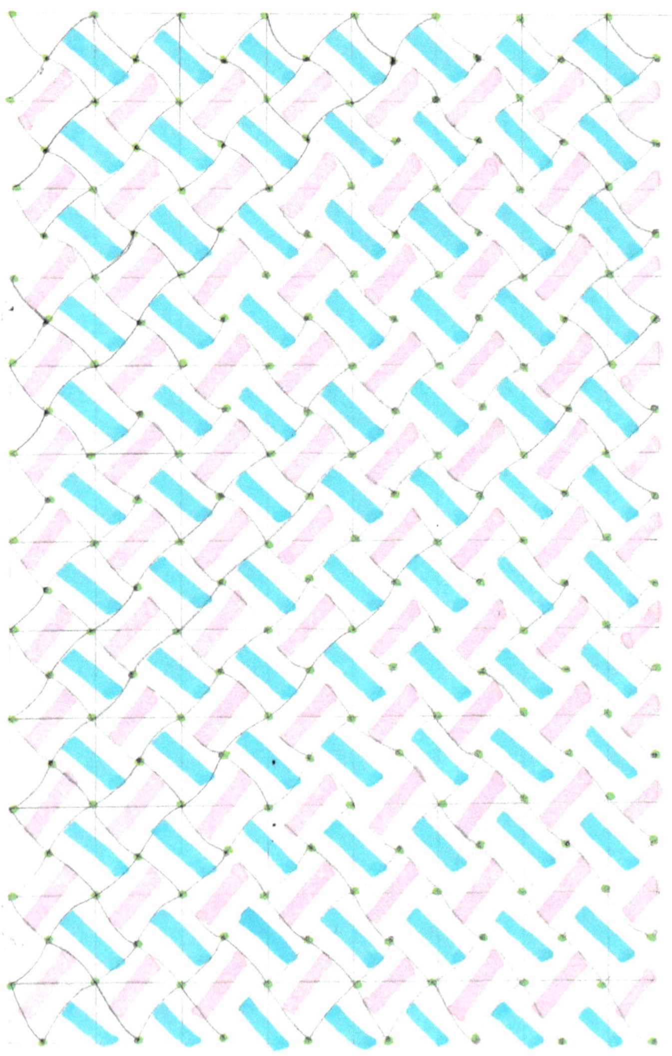

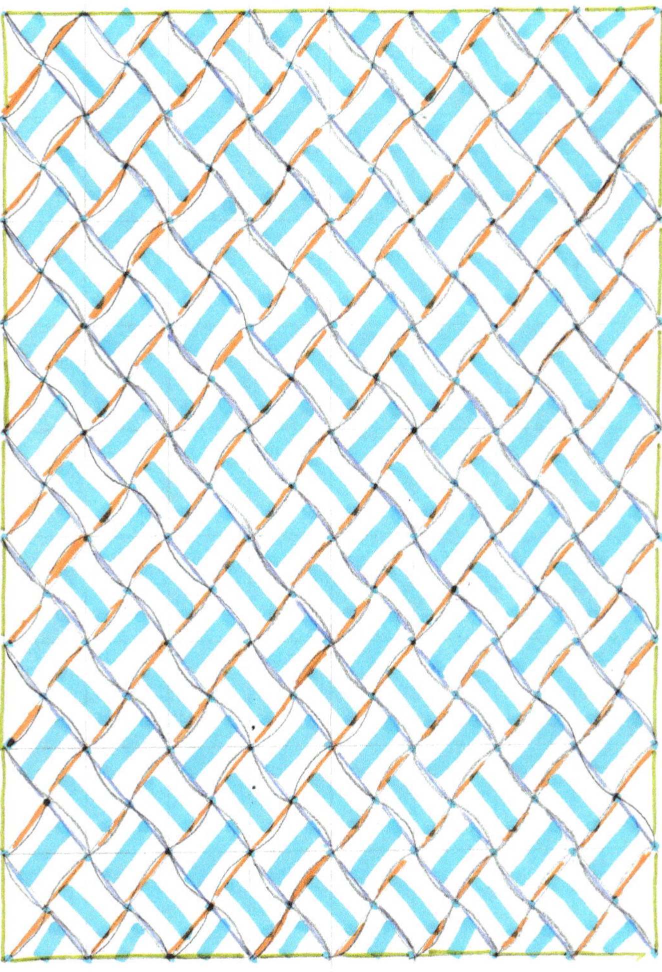

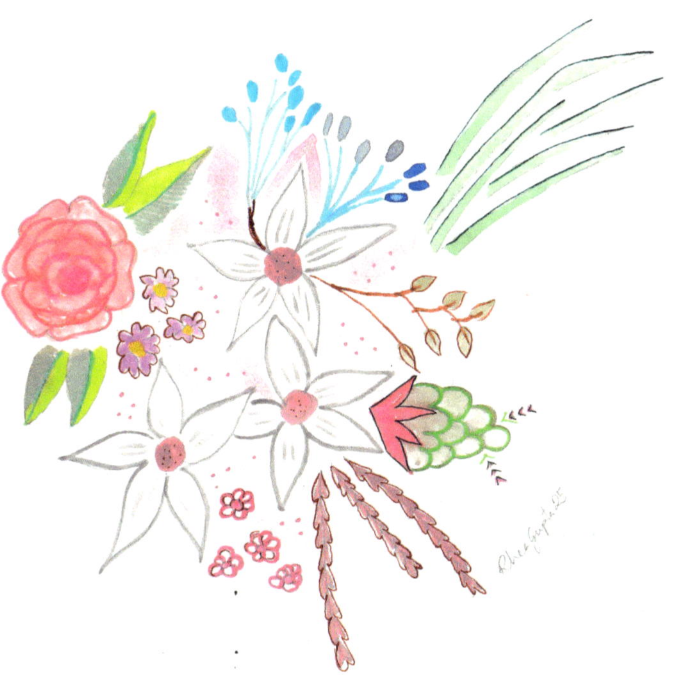

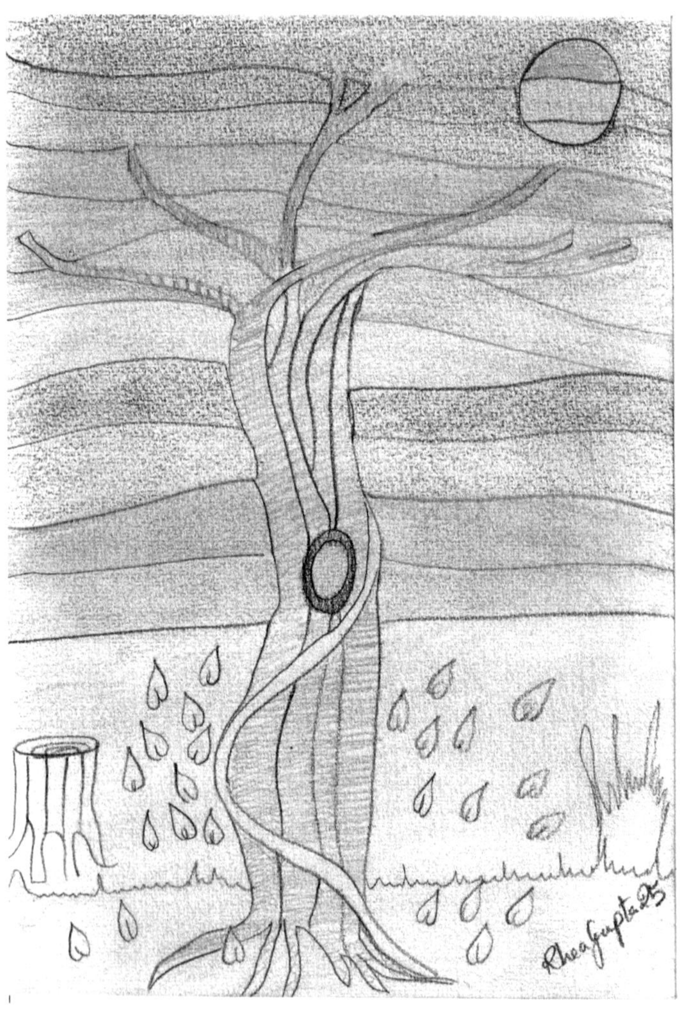

Roses, Mud & Water

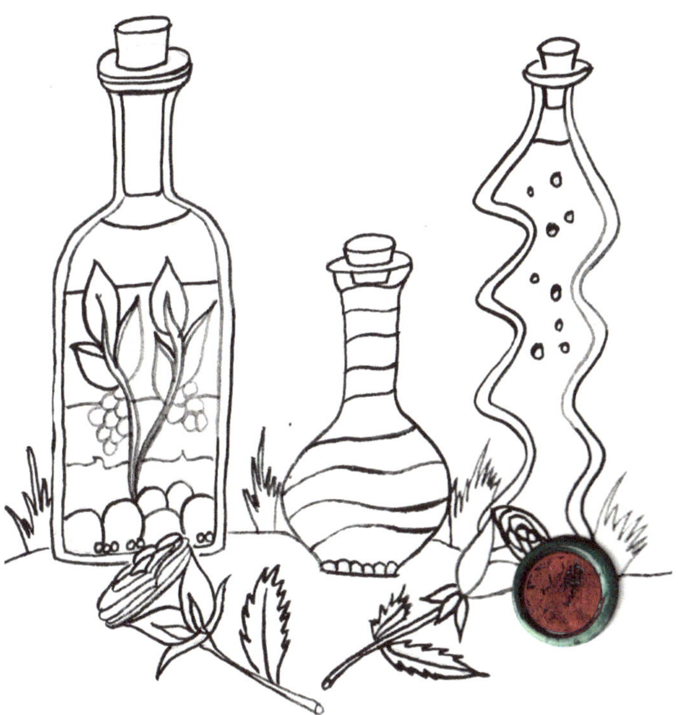

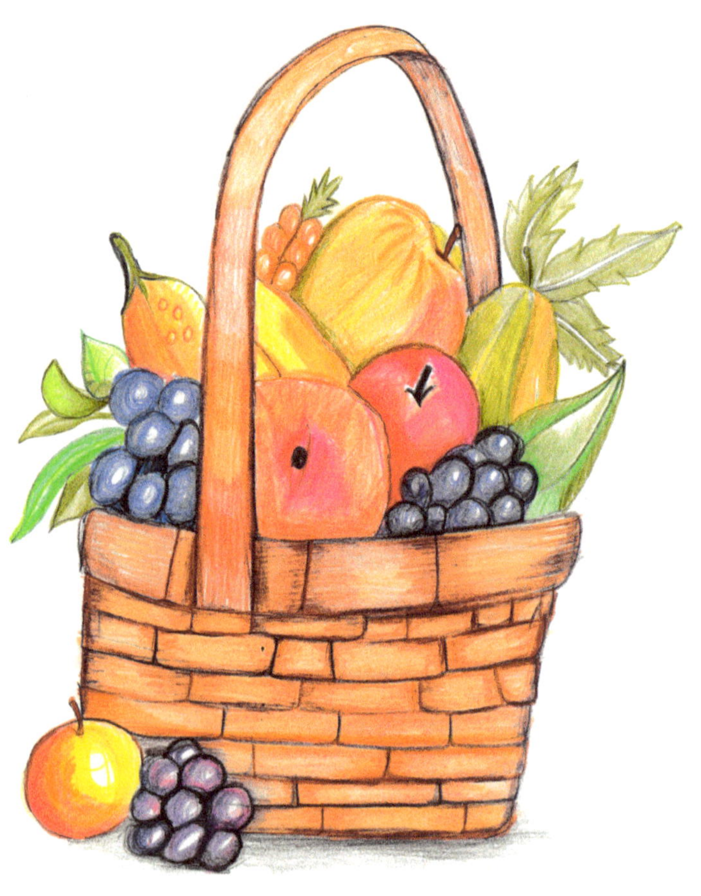

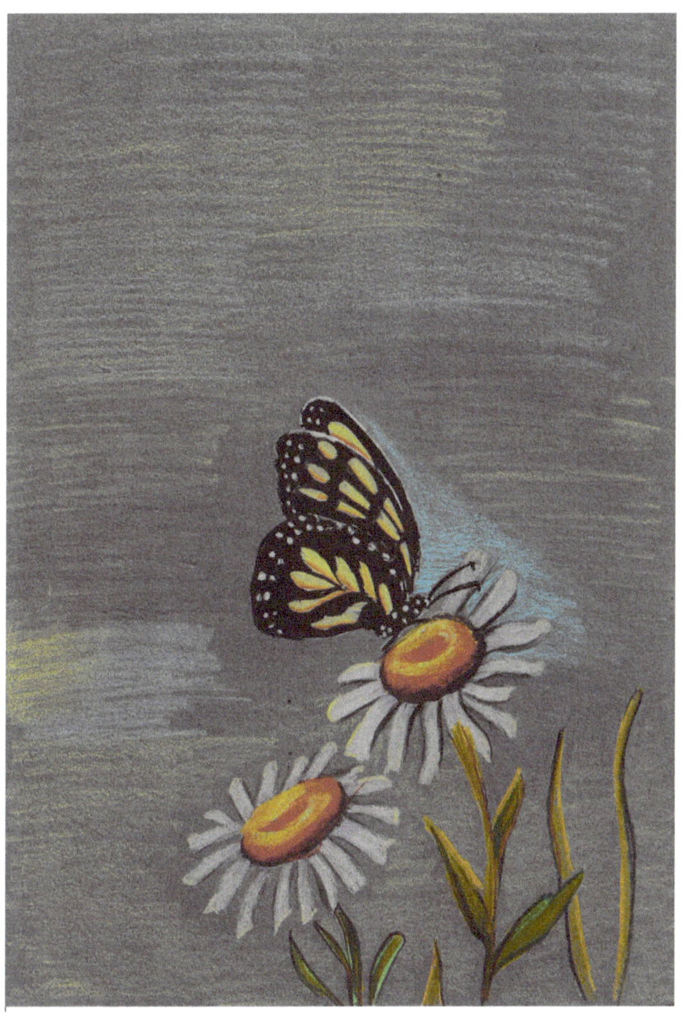

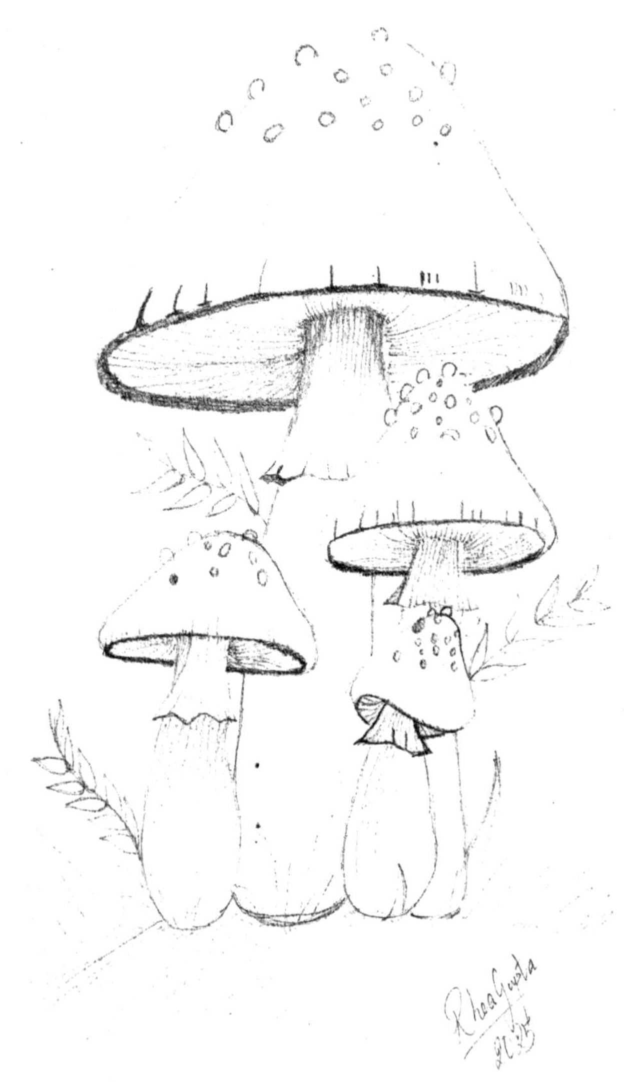

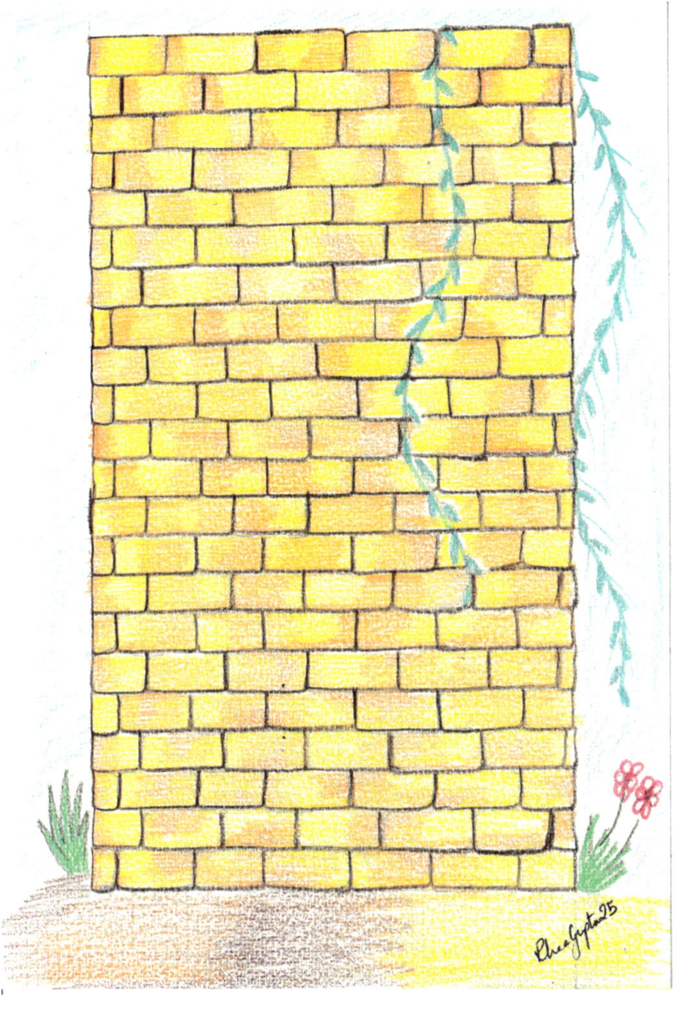

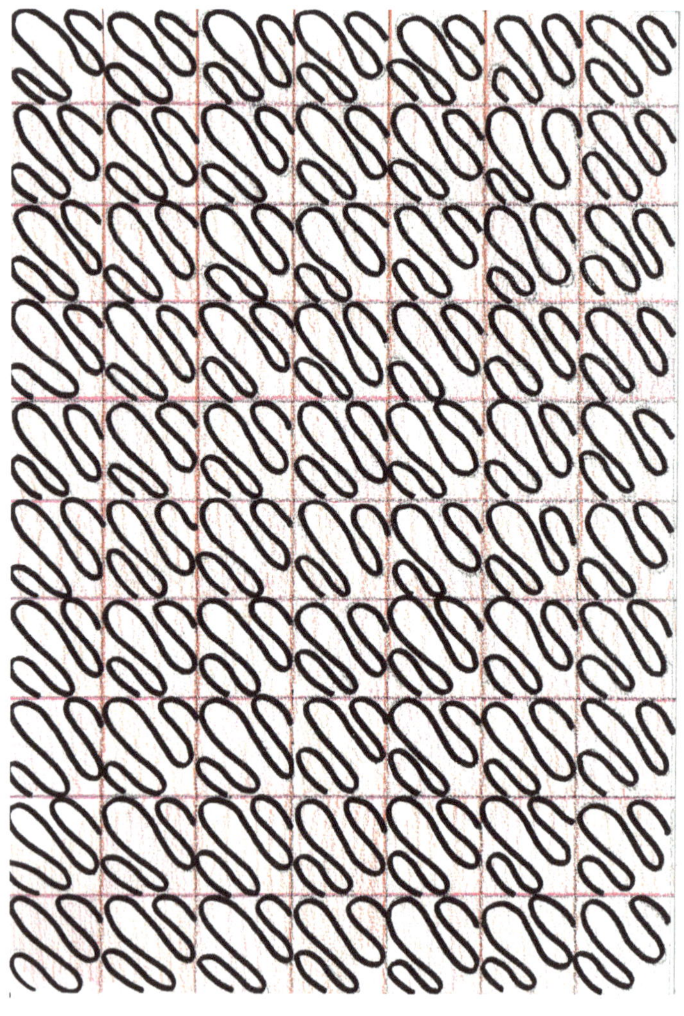

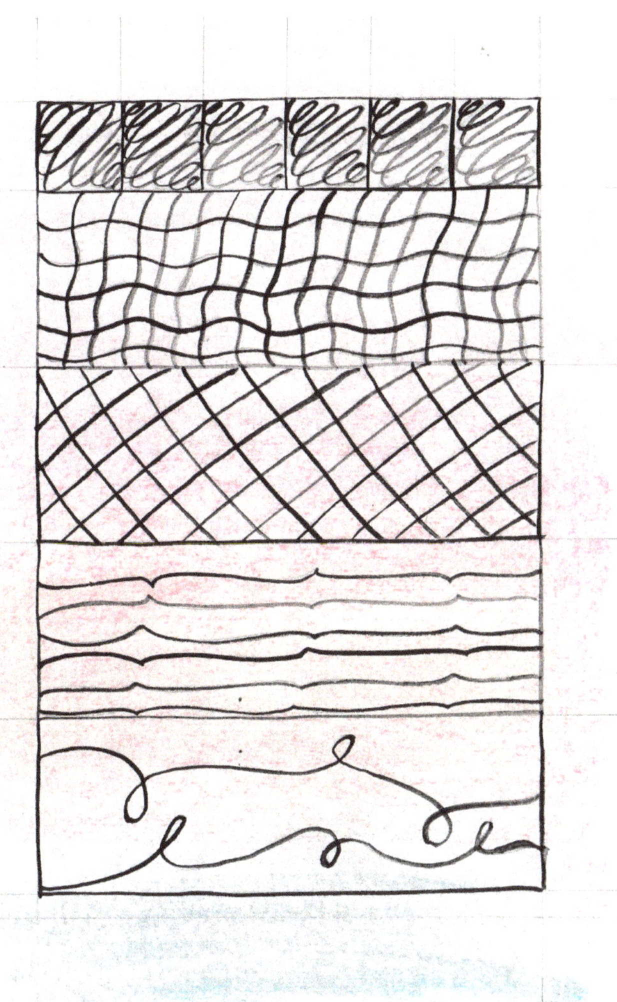

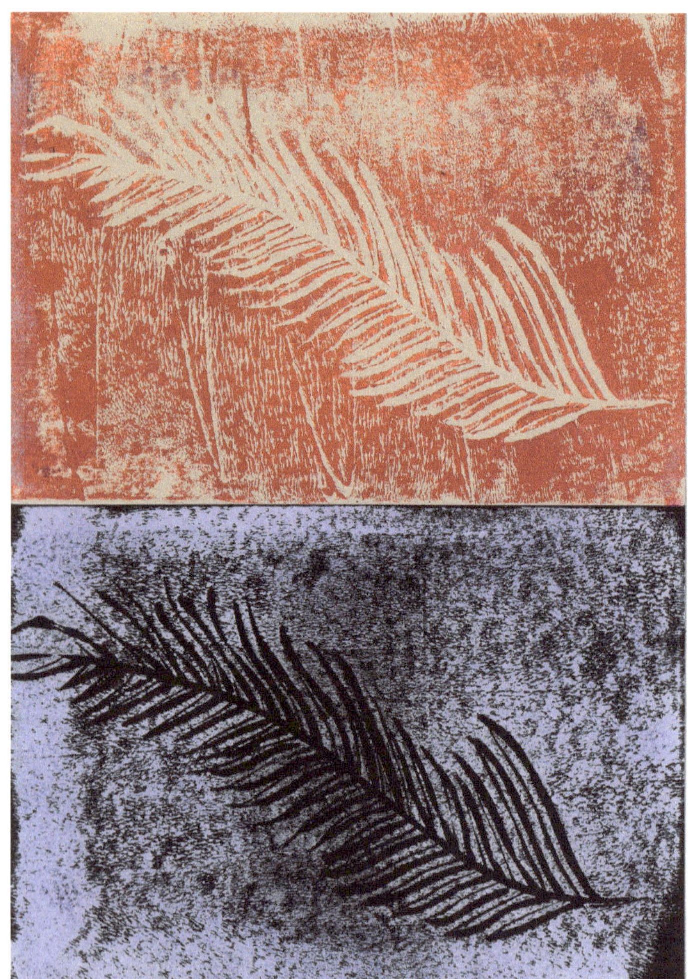

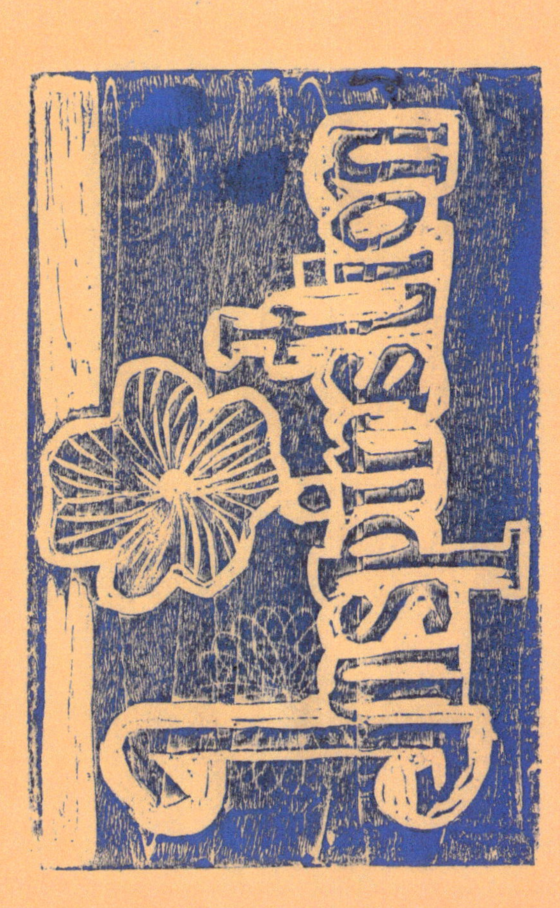

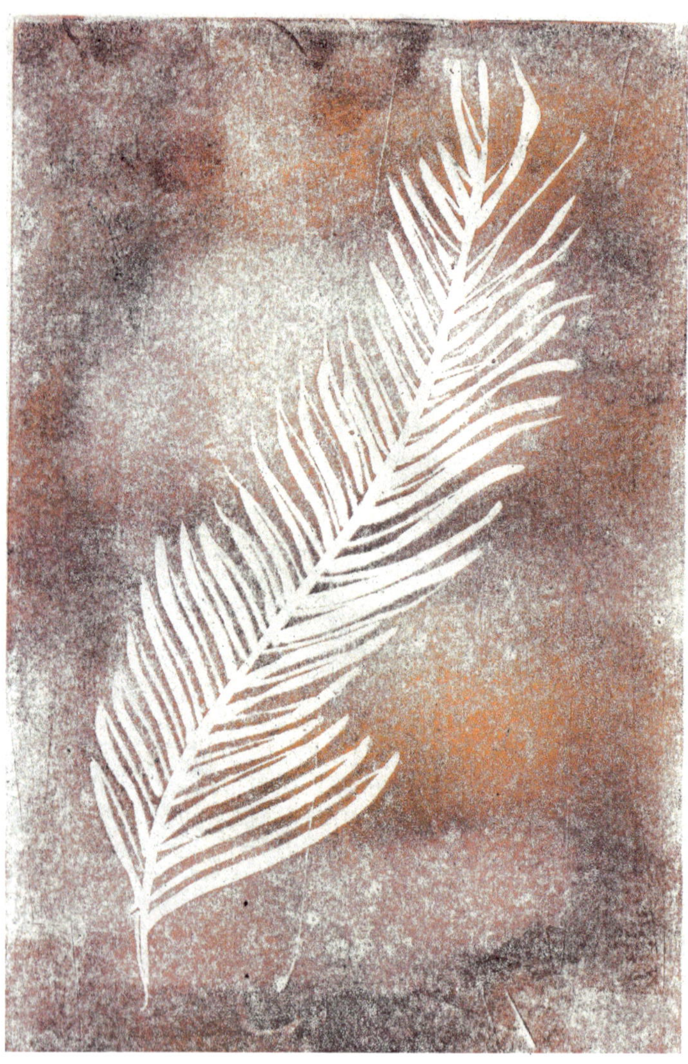

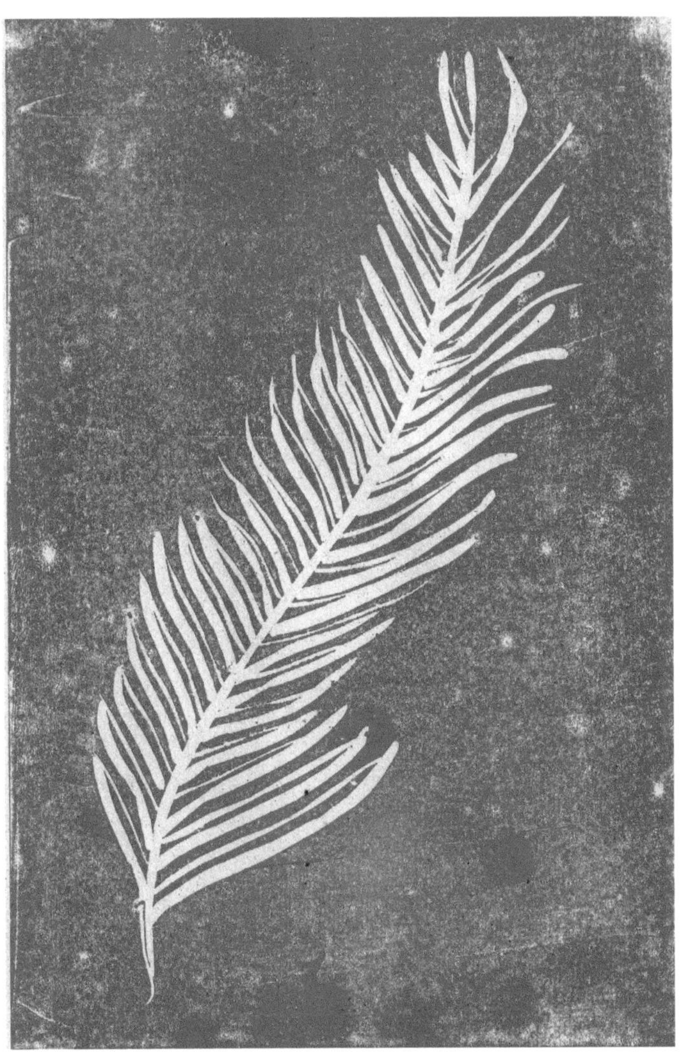

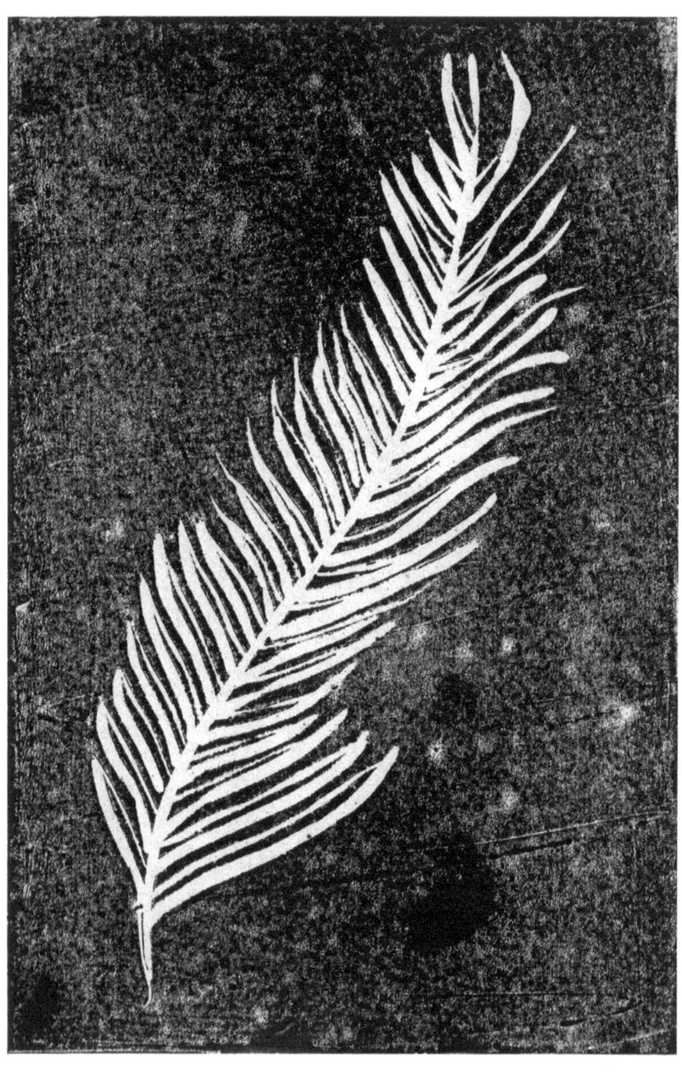

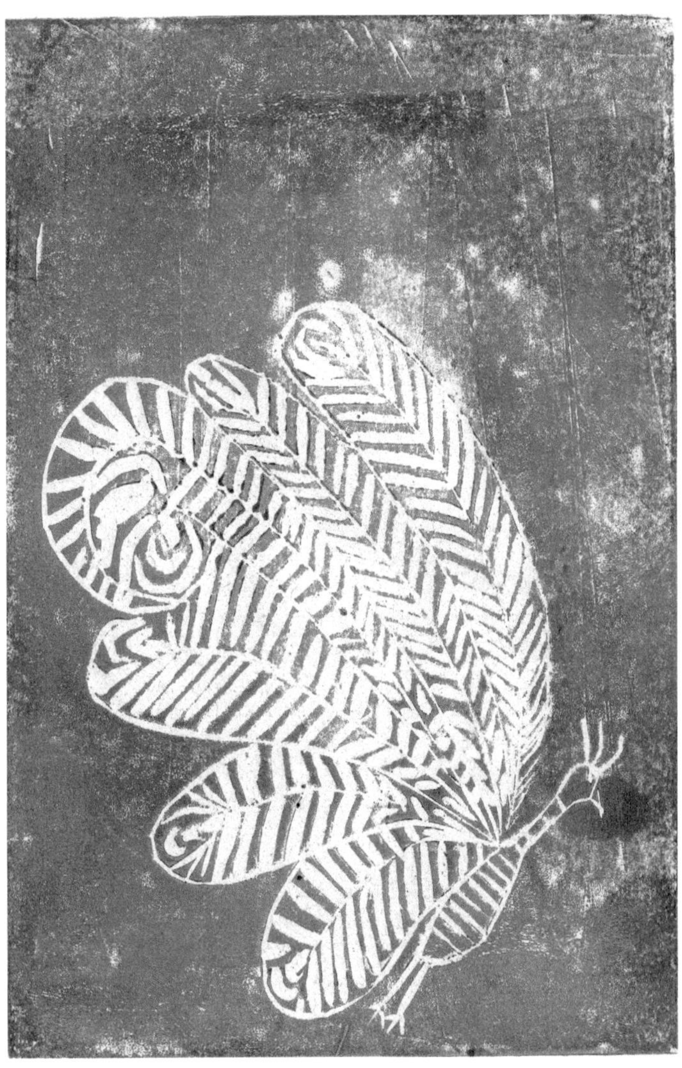

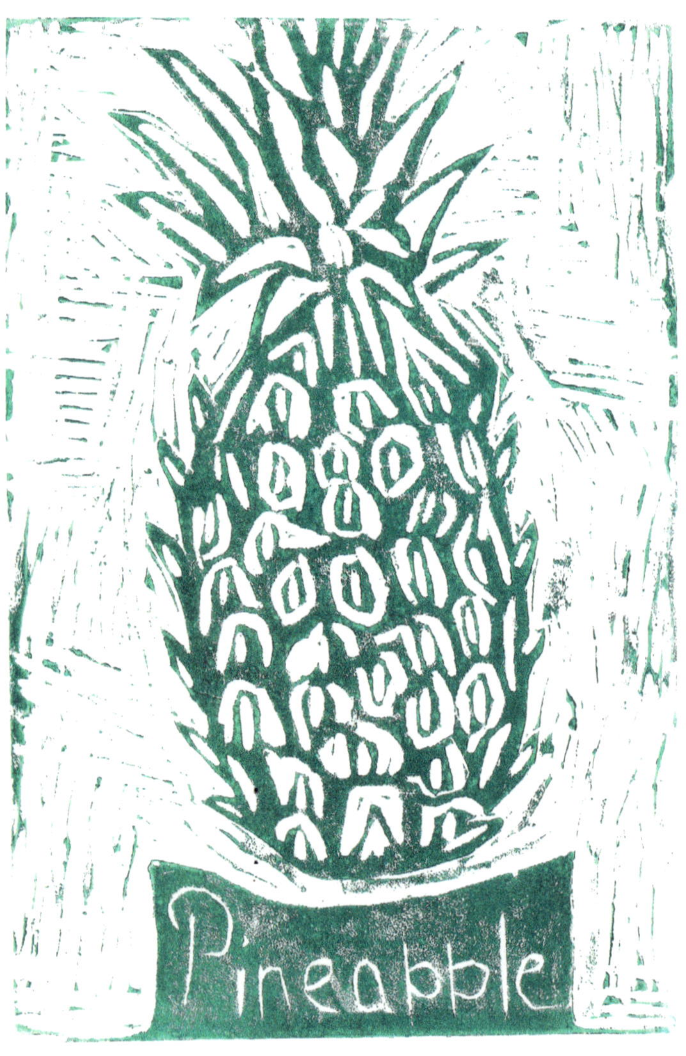
Pineabble